AN ALBUM
OF THE
VIETNAM WAR

AN ALBUM OF THE VIETNAM WAR

BY DON LAWSON

FRANKLIN WATTS 1986
NEW YORK LONDON TORONTO SYDNEY

Library of Congress Cataloging in Publication Data

Lawson, Don.
An album of the Vietnam War.

Includes index.
Summary: An illustrated history, with emphasis on
American involvement, of the war in Vietnam from
Ho Chi Minh's declaration of independence to the
withdrawal of United States troops.
1. Vietnamese Conflict, 1961–1975—United States—
Juvenile literature. [1. Vietnamese Conflict,
1961–1975] I. Title.
DS558.L378 1986   959.704′33′73   85-26624
ISBN 0-531-10139-8

CONTENTS

CHAPTER ONE
HOW THE VIETNAM WAR BEGAN
1

CHAPTER TWO
THE UNITED STATES
ENTERS THE VIETNAM WAR
10

CHAPTER THREE
FIGHTING THE VIETNAM WAR
28

CHAPTER FOUR
THE WAR ON THE HOME FRONT
62

CHAPTER FIVE
THE FINAL ACT
71

INDEX
86

AN ALBUM
OF THE
VIETNAM WAR

CHINA
Dien Bien Phu
Haiphong
Hanoi
Red River
Mekong River
Gulf of Tonkin
HAINAN
L A O S
V I E T N A M
Vientiane
17th parallel / Demilitarized Zone (1954)
Khe Sanh
Hue
Da Nang
THAILAND
Mekong River
Ho Chi Minh Trail
Dakto
Bangkok
KAMPUCHEA
(CAMBODIA)
Pleiku
Cam Ranh Bay
Phnom Penh
Saigon
(now Ho Chi Minh City)
Gulf of Thailand
Mekong Delta
South China Sea
VIETNAM

HOW THE VIETNAM WAR BEGAN

When World War II began in Europe in 1939, several of the nations involved in that conflict controlled colonial empires, or other, smaller countries throughout the world. One of the biggest of these colonial empires belonged to France, which controlled countries in Africa and Southeast Asia. France's Southeast Asian colony was called French Indochina. French Indochina occupied part of the large peninsula extending southward from China into the South China Sea. It included Vietnam and Vietnam's neighbors to the west, Cambodia (now Kampuchea) and Laos.

By the end of the war in 1945, most of the colonial empires had been broken up, and the colonies were promised their independence. But France did not want to give up its overseas empire. Its colonies had been great sources of wealth before the war, and now they were needed more than ever to help rebuild France after the destruction of World War II. France was ready to fight to regain control of its former colonies. But the people of the former colonies were also ready to fight—for their independence.

In Africa the French fought for many years before reluctantly giving up the struggle and granting their former African colonies their independence. In Indochina the French also met with fierce resistance from the people of northern Vietnam.

Vietnam had long struggled to be independent, not only from France but from every other country as well. In 1941, soon after Japan entered World War II by bombing the American naval base at Pearl Harbor, Hawaii, it began a quick conquest of the whole of Southeast Asia. Among the territories it conquered was Indochina. The French offered little resistance, cooperating with the Japanese, but they were still driven out late in the war. Although the Vietnamese were glad to see the French go, they soon realized that they had only traded one ruling nation for another. At the end of World War II, Japan surrendered to the United States and left Vietnam. Many Vietnamese were determined not to submit again to any foreign rule.

HO CHI MINH AND THE VIETMINH The Vietnamese resistance movement was called the *Vietminh*, or Vietnam Independence League. The leader of the Vietminh was a fiery Communist revolutionary named Ho Chi Minh. On September 2, 1945, Ho Chi Minh and his supporters declared independence and established a new government with headquarters at Hanoi in northern Vietnam. Called the Democratic Republic of Vietnam (DRV), there was very little that was democratic about it, however. The DRV was a one-party Communist dictatorship with Ho at the helm.

A few months after the founding of the DRV the French tried to regain Indochina. They met little resistance in once again taking possession of Laos and Cambodia. In the southern part of Vietnam they also reestablished themselves without much bloodshed.

But as soon as they began to move north they ran into resistance from Vietminh troops. For a time the French tried to negotiate a peaceful takeover of the whole country, but when these negotiations collapsed scattered fighting again broke out. In late 1946 fighting developed between the French forces and those of the Vietminh.

Actually, no outside observers thought that the French would have any trouble defeating the Vietminh, whom they outnumbered at least three to one. But a brilliant Vietminh general, Vo Nguyen Giap, used a method of fighting that made the size difference of the opposing forces unimportant. It was called *guerrilla warfare*. (*Guerrilla* is a Spanish word meaning "little war.")

In many ways guerrilla warfare was similar to the fighting tactics used by the American Indians against the U.S. Cavalry on the western plains in the nineteenth century. Guerrilla bands were small, compact fighting units that specialized in surprise hit-and-run attacks. Appearing suddenly almost out of nowhere, the Vietminh guerrillas would shoot or knife half-a-dozen or more advancing French troops and then disappear into the covering underbrush, perhaps tossing a few hand grenades behind them as they left. And the Vietminh had one big advantage that the American Indians never had; most of the Vietnam countryside was covered with thick tropical jungle where guerrillas could hide before an attack and escape afterward.

Early in the conflict between the French and the Vietminh, the French quickly gained control of most of the major cities and population centers in the south. But they never were able to control the vast rural countryside, and it was there that Giap's guerrillas could hide among the villagers or lie in wait along jungle trails and ambush the French as they tried to move north. Again and again the French tried to meet the Vietminh in a major battle, where their superior troop strength and their superior firepower would have meant certain defeat for the Vietminh. But Giap would not allow such a situation to develop.

In this frustrating and indecisive fashion the French Indochina War dragged on for months and finally for years with neither side able to gain the upper hand. At home in France—as casualty lists continued to grow and the end seemed nowhere in sight—a rising tide of criticism began to threaten the government. In Vietnam the Vietminh seemed determined to continue its guerrilla fighting for another ten or even twenty years if that was what was necessary to drive out the French and permanently establish Vietnam's independence.

THE BATTLE OF DIEN BIEN PHU   Finally, partially in desperation, the French military command decided to present the Vietminh with an opportunity for a major, traditional, head-on, full-scale infantry battle that it could not possibly refuse. Once such an engagement took place, the French believed, the Vietminh would be overwhelmed, their main fighting force destroyed, and the war would be over.

The place decided upon by the French to lay this trap was called Dien Bien Phu, meaning "big frontier administration center." It was situated in a valley in northern Vietnam near the border of Laos. To get there the French had to drop troops and supplies by parachute. The first troops built an airstrip, and soon artillery and small tanks were being ferried into Dien Bien Phu in huge transport planes. Additional troops were also ferried in until the French garrison numbered some 16,000 men. Their commander was General Henri Navarre, an outstanding veteran of World War II.

The French military command was right about one thing: General Giap and his Vietminh forces would attempt a frontal assault on Dien Bien Phu. But the French were wrong about almost everything else. First, General Navarre seriously underestimated the number of troops General Giap would be able to assemble for a Vietminh attack. By early 1954, a few months after the first French paratroopers had landed at Dien Bien Phu, they were surrounded by some 50,000 Vietminh soldiers. Navarre also expected the battle for the fortified camp to be a short one. Once the Vietminh committed themselves to battle, he planned a sharp counterattack that would overrun the Vietminh positions. But General Giap had no such plans. He intended to lay siege to Dien Bien Phu, punishing its garrison with artillery bombardments until it was severely weakened. Then he planned to make his direct assault.

The French also miscalculated in the matter of supplies. They depended on being supplied by continuous airdrops while the Vietminh—who had no air transport—would have the apparently impossible task of hauling in its supplies along jungle trails. What Giap and the Vietminh did have, however, was literally thousands of civilians who were ready, willing, and able to act as human pack animals to keep them well supplied with food and ammunition—especially artillery shells. It remained to be seen whether airdrops could keep the French adequately supplied during a long siege.

General Navarre's two top aides were Colonel Christian de Castries and Lieutenant Colonel Pierre Langlais. When Navarre decided all was in readiness at Dien Bien Phu, he flew back to Saigon in southern Vietnam and left de Castries and Langlais in charge. Because Navarre had predicted that the Vietminh would attack as soon as he left, the two commanders placed their troops on a twenty-four hour alert.

Ho Chi Minh, center, and his commanders, planning the battle of Dien Bien Phu, 1954. General Vo Nguyen Giap is to the right, in white.

The French trenches at Dien Bien Phu. The Vietminh shelled the French garrison from surrounding hills, forcing the French to survive in World War I-like trenches. The Vietminh were able to penetrate the garrison by digging tunnels.

But no attack came. The French waited, and waited—and waited. Giap's delay was a psychological weapon to weaken French morale. Giap was also waiting for bad weather to set in, when rain and fog would prevent French flyers from landing at or taking off from Dien Bien Phu. Giap knew such weather always descended on this particular area in the early spring. And the weather forecast proved correct once again.

Finally, in mid-March 1954, with the Dien Bien Phu fortified positions shrouded in fog and mist, General Giap unleashed a massive artillery bombardment. Both its timing and its ferocity took the French garrison completely by surprise. But the French were veteran soldiers, too, and they rallied to fight off the ground attack they expected would immediately follow the long artillery barrage. This time they were not disappointed.

The Vietminh infantry attacked in human waves, suffering severe casualties but continuing their advance. Finally the French beat them off and mounted a counterattack. The Vietminh in turn beat off the French inflicting severe casualties on them. Obviously the battle would not be decided quickly.

As a matter of fact, the battle almost immediately settled into a siege that continued through the rest of March and on into April. As the siege wore on, the French military command began to realize that their forces were trapped at Dien Bien Phu and that they had no way to relieve them. At this point the French government in Paris began to look around for outside help. One of the first sources it looked to was the United States, which has been France's ally in World War II.

AMERICA'S EARLY ROLE IN VIETNAM

Up to this time the United States had been supporting France's efforts to regain Indochina—not with troops but with money and war supplies. It has been estimated that the United States was paying as much as 75 percent of the French military costs in Vietnam. Now, however, France wanted the United States to launch an air strike or series of air strikes against the Vietminh at Dien Bien Phu. Such air strikes could come from aircraft carriers in the South China Sea or perhaps from nearby Thailand, where the United States had air bases. There was even some hint that the United States might drop an atom bomb on Hanoi, as it had dropped atom bombs on Hiroshima and Nagasaki to end World War II, to end the French Indochina War with equal decisiveness.

The basic reason the United States had been supporting France's struggle in Indochina was that Ho Chi Minh and many of the Vietminh were Communists. The Communists, the U.S. government believed, were not just trying to establish an independent government in Vietnam. What they were really trying to do was take over the whole of Southeast Asia. Thus, they reasoned that if Vietnam were allowed to fall to Ho Chi Minh and the Vietminh, probably all the other nations of Southeast Asia would also fall to the Communists. This idea was central to the so-called domino theory held by U.S. President Dwight D. Eisenhower and other government officials.

Supporting the domino theory was the fact that both the Soviet Union and China were backing Ho Chi Minh and his government. They were doing so just as the United States was doing with France—not with troops but with money and war supplies. During World War II the Soviet Union and China had been on the Allied side against Germany, Italy, and Japan. Since the end of the war, however, the Soviet Union had taken over several formerly independent countries in Eastern Europe, and the United States was convinced that the Soviets were determined to rule the world. In 1949, after a long civil war, the Chinese Communists had gained control of China and had since become allies of the Soviet Union in its efforts to spread Communism in Asia. If such expansion was to be stopped, the United States believed, it had to be stopped in Vietnam.

Harry S. Truman, the first post–World War II American president, had been the first top U.S. official who tried to prevent Communist expansion in Southeast Asia by supporting French efforts to regain Indochina. Truman's successor, President Eisenhower, had increased this support. Now, however, Eisenhower was not prepared to take the United States as far as France wanted in defeating the Vietminh at Dien Bien Phu. For one thing, Eisenhower (or ''Ike'' as he was popularly known) did not want to bring China and the Soviet Union into the war and did not want American troops involved in a land war on the vast Asian continent. A former general himself—he had commanded the Allied forces that invaded France in 1944 and defeated Germany in 1945—Ike believed such involvement in Asia would be suicidal because the fighting might drag on for a generation.

Consequently, when General Paul Ely, chief of staff of the French army, flew to Washington, D.C., at the height of the battle of Dien Bien Phu, his request for an American air strike against the Vietminh was refused. Ely's request was given serious consideration—Secretary of State John Foster Dulles favored further aid and the Joint Chiefs of Staff even drew up plans for U.S. combat against the Vietminh—but Ike had the last word, and the word was no.

When word reached the Dien Bien Phu defenders that the United States had refused further aid, they knew the end was inevitable. Nevertheless, they fought on valiantly for many weeks. At the end of the first week of May 1954, General Giap mounted a mass attack that overran the French garrison, whose remaining members were finally forced to surrender after hand-to-hand combat.

Within a matter of days the French had left Indochina for good. But the United States was not prepared to let the Vietminh take over all of Vietnam. The south was not yet under the control of Ho Chi Minh's forces, and there was evidence that it did not want to be. Instead of getting out of Vietnam along with the French, the United States began to offer massive support to the people of the south to continue their fight against a Communist takeover of the entire nation.

*The Vietminh raising
their flag of victory
over Dien Bien Phu*

2

THE UNITED STATES ENTERS THE VIETNAM WAR

After the French defeat at Dien Bien Phu an international peace conference was held at Geneva, Switzerland. At this conference it was decided to divide Vietnam at the 17th parallel of latitude. On either side of this division line there was to be a narrow demilitarized zone (DMZ) where no troops would be allowed. Ho Chi Minh's government was given control of all territory north of the DMZ. The State of Vietnam, or South Vietnam, was given control of all territory south of the DMZ.

This division of Vietnam was only supposed to last for two years. After that free elections would be held to decide whether to reunite the country and what kind of government all the people of Vietnam wanted. The United States reluctantly accepted this temporary arrangement and immediately began to pour food and military aid into South Vietnam. In addition, President Eisenhower authorized several hundred U.S. military advisers to help train the South Vietnam army. (Sending these advisers eventually proved to be exactly what Ike had earlier opposed—involvement of U.S. troops in an Asian land war.)

The additional food supplies were badly needed by South Vietnam, because as soon as the division of Vietnam was announced a million North Vietnamese began to flood into South Vietnam. U.S. government observers said these refu-

A Vietminh victory parade staged by occupying troops in Hanoi, 1954

Vietnamese refugees fleeing northern Vietnam, 1954. A large number of the nearly one million refugees were Catholic. Here, a U.S. Navy ship prepares to take some of the refugees on board. Many also fled overland to South Vietnam.

President of South Vietnam, Ngo Dinh Diem, in his palace in Saigon

gees were fleeing the Communist government of North Vietnam. This was partially true, because most of the refugees were Catholic and the Communists were officially opposed to all forms of religion. Also important was the question of a permanent food supply. South Vietnam had long been known as the "rice bowl" of Indochina, and its rice fields in the Mekong River delta were among the richest in the world. By contrast, the rice fields in the Red River delta of North Vietnam, near Hanoi, were annually flooded by spring monsoon rains. The United States might be a temporary source of food, but as a permanent source the Vietnamese looked to the Mekong Delta rice fields.

Although the Catholic refugees from North Vietnam created a temporary problem for the South Vietnamese government and its U.S. ally, they helped to resolve another and perhaps more important matter. The United States was trying to help establish some sort of stable government in South Vietnam, and the leader they looked to was a man named Ngo Dinh Diem. A staunch foe of the Communists, Diem appealed to the United States. But he was also a Catholic, and most of the Vietnamese people were Buddhists. With the support of the Catholic refugees from North Vietnam as well as support from the U:S., Diem succeeded in becoming president of the Republic of South Vietnam when it was established in 1955.

Soon after he became president of the new republic, Diem made it clear that he had no intention of letting South Vietnam take part in national elections—as had been agreed at Geneva—to decide what form of government should be established throughout the country. Although Ho Chi Minh's DRV kept calling for national elections, Diem stubbornly refused such demands. Diem's refusal was supported by U.S. officials because they agreed that the North Vietnamese Communists would not allow truly free elections. They would simply order their people to vote for Communist rule over a reunified Vietnam. There was also some fear that many South Vietnamese would vote to join North Vietnam.

As the reunification stalemate continued, Diem built up the Army of the Republic of Vietnam (ARVN) to some 150,000 men. As ARVN grew, so did its auxiliary of American military advisers. By the end of President Eisenhower's term in office in 1961 there were more than 2,000 U.S. military advisers in South Vietnam.

Meanwhile, Ho Chi Minh's Vietminh forces had not been inactive. Many of them had remained in South Vietnam after the Geneva agreement. Soon they began guerrilla actions against the ARVN forces, just like those they had previously carried out against the French. In addition, General Giap sent other guerrilla units from North Vietnam into South Vietnam in an attempt to overthrow the Diem regime.

In 1960 all of the former Vietminh guerrillas as well as many of their civilian sympathizers in the South were formed into an organization known as the National Liberation Front (NLF). Later members of the NLF became known as the Vietcong meaning Vietnamese Communists. The Vietcong was separate from the regular North Vietnam army, which remained in North Vietnam until later in the war.

As Vietcong activity against the Diem regime steadily increased, so did American military support. When John F. Kennedy succeeded Eisenhower as president in 1961, he almost immediately dispatched a number of Special Forces troops, popularly known as Green Berets, as combat advisers to Vietnam. In addition, Kennedy sent many armed helicopters piloted by Americans. In time the skies over Vietnam became so filled with helicopters, or choppers, that the conflict became known as the chopper war. Within two years after Kennedy took office some 15,000 members of the American military forces were in Vietnam.

EARLY ROLE OF THE GREEN BERETS

Since the United States was not officially at war with North Vietnam, American Special Forces, or Green Berets, were not actually supposed to fight the Vietcong. Nevertheless they did engage in combat, and there were U.S. military casualties as early as 1961. The Green Berets—so-called because of their distinctive headgear—were trained in antiguerrilla warfare. Skilled in jungle fighting and sabotage, they taught in turn these skills to ARVN troops. Then they led these troops against the Vietcong in jungle engagements that amounted to guerrillas fighting guerrillas.

To keep the American public from knowing that some of their troops were in fact already at war, the Green Berets were reported to be involved in "counter-insurgency activity." The Vietcong were the insurgents and the Green Berets were simply countering their efforts.

*An American Special Forces soldier giving
medical attention to a Vietnamese villager*

President Kennedy and his two principal advisers on Vietnam, Secretary of Defense Robert McNamara (with glasses) and Secretary of State Dean Rusk

Left: helicopters in flight over Vietnam's Mekong Delta. Right: an American adviser instructs South Vietnamese soldiers in bayonet technique.

In the mountainous highlands of the interior of South Vietnam there were tribes known as Montagnards. The Green Berets enlisted the Montagnards as jungle fighters and led them in hit-and-run raids against the Vietcong. Later in the war, as the number of Green Berets increased, they also fought secretly in neighboring Laos. Near the end of the war, when the United States decided to remove all of its troops from Vietnam and let ARVN forces do the fighting the Montagnards were simply abandoned. When the North Vietnamese waged an extermination campaign against them, this resulted in their virtual destruction as a people.

THE DOWNFALL OF DIEM

Despite Green Beret and ARVN antiguerrilla or counter-insurgency efforts, however, the Vietcong continued to threaten the overthrow of the Diem regime. In these efforts they were supported by many South Vietnamese civilians who resented Diem's dictatorial methods. Peasants objected particularly to Diem's failure to keep his promises of land reform throughout South Vietnam. These were supposed to bring the redistribution of farmland to the rural population, but such reforms never came.

There were also widespread rumors of graft and corruption in the Diem government in Saigon. Diem's brother and chief adviser, Ngo Dinh Nhu, was accused of taking bribes to grant important jobs and political favors. Nhu's wife was not only involved in corrupt practices in the capital but was also a sworn enemy of the growing Buddhist movement. Widely known as the Dragon Lady, Madame Nhu publicly announced her approval of suicides by several Buddhist priests who set themselves on fire in protest against the policies of the increasingly dictatorial Diem government.

As the protest grew in South Vietnam (with even some ARVN elements threatening to revolt) the Kennedy administration in Washington decided that Diem must go. Once top ARVN generals received word—probably passed to them by the U.S. Central Intelligence Agency (CIA)—that the United States would not object to a political coup to remove Diem, they went into immediate action. Early in November 1963, President Diem and his brother were assassinated by ARVN generals who then took control of the South Vietnamese government.

Above: *Montagnards from the highlands of Vietnam leaving their villages.* Left: *President Diem's brother, Ngo Dinh Nhu.* Right: *President Diem's sister-in-law, Madame Ngo Dinh Nhu, considered herself South Vietnam's First Lady. American advisers to Diem considered her a troublemaker.*

Rebel troops taking over Diem's palace in the 1963 coup which toppled the South Vietnamese president and his brother from power

Passersby stop to watch as flames envelop a Buddhist monk, one of several ritual suicides to protest Diem's anti-Buddhist policies. Of the suicides, Madame Nhu had proclaimed, "Let them burn, and we shall clap our hands." She also referred to the burnings as "barbecues."

Three weeks after Diem's death President Kennedy was assassinated in Dallas, Texas. (There was no connection between the two assassinations). Kennedy was succeeded in office by Vice President Lyndon Baines Johnson, who also succeeded in getting the United States still more deeply involved in the Vietnam War.

 When Johnson took office as president he was keenly interested in improving economic and social conditions in the United States, including the passage of important civil rights legislation. (His domestic program was called the Great Society.) At the same time he was seriously concerned about foreign affairs, especially the threatened loss of Vietnam, which might trigger the loss of the whole of Southeast Asia. Like the several presidents who had preceded him in office—Truman, Eisenhower, and Kennedy—and the one who would succeed him—Richard M. Nixon—Johnson was a firm believer in the domino theory.

The Vietnam conflict presented Johnson with a major problem: How was he to carry out his Great Society program at home, which called for huge federal expenditures, and at the same time continue to give unlimited military support to South Vietnam, which would also be enormously expensive? There seemed to be only two possible answers to this problem: get the United States out of its Vietnam commitment or cut back on the domestic program. But Johnson believed that abandoning South Vietnam would be cowardly and shortsighted where U.S. foreign affairs goals were concerned. And abandoning the Great Society program would mean turning his back on everything he had ever stood for as a public official.

In the end President Johnson decided to try to provide both guns and butter. He would give unstinting aid to South Vietnam, and he would also proceed with Great Society social welfare legislation. The final result of this decision was carrying on a war against North Vietnam while trying to deceive the American public into thinking its military forces were not actually engaged in that war. The first step along this path of deception was getting Congress to pass the Tonkin Gulf Resolution on August 7, 1964.

According to the Constitution, only Congress can declare war. In certain short-term emergency situations, however, the president does have specific rights to commit American troops

President Johnson (right) discussing Vietnam with Senator Fulbright, Chairman of the Senate Foreign Relations Commitee

A chopper landing along the Ho Chi Minh Trail (1964)

64
62

to combat. In Vietnam, President Johnson used those emergency powers to the limit. And for a period of several months he was responsible for a secret American war against North Vietnam.

After the assassination of President Diem a series of men tried to take over control of the South Vietnamese government. None ruled more than a few months. Finally General Nguyen Van Thieu came to power and the U.S. government backed him to the hilt, not only as a "permanent" president but also in his attempts to drive the Vietcong out of South Vietnam.

In support of the South Vietnamese army President Johnson authorized what amounted to a secret aerial war on the Vietcong. American pilots flew reconnaissance missions over Vietcong territory, with orders to fire back only if fired on. Such orders were obviously impossible to enforce. If an American pilot saw an enemy plane, he didn't wait to be fired on. He fired first and answered questions afterward, and the answer was always, "Yes, of course I was fired on."

American transport planes also flew Green Beret guerrillas into combat areas, and American bombers carried out covert (secret) missions against North Vietnam targets. U.S. Navy destroyers patrolled the North Vietnamese coast and supported South Vietnamese seaborne guerrillas on raids against North Vietnamese onshore naval bases. It was during one such U.S.–supported naval mission that an incident occurred—or was said to have occurred—in the Gulf of Tonkin.

At the end of July 1964 South Vietnamese patrol torpedo (PT) boats raided North Vietnamese naval bases. On August 2, while patrolling the Gulf of Tonkin near where the South Vietnamese raid had taken place, the U.S. destroyer *Maddox* was reportedly fired on by North Vietnamese PT boats. The *Maddox* was undamaged, but its skipper, Captain John J. Herrick, reported the incident via radio to Washington. The next

*Cargo choppers taking off
from a supply ship off the
coast of South Vietnam*

day the *Maddox* was ordered back on patrol duty in the same waters. This time she was accompanied by a second U.S. destroyer, the *C. Turner Joy.*

August 3 passed without incident, but on the night of August 4 Captain Herrick radioed Washington that both the *Maddox* and *C. Turner Joy* were under attack by North Vietnamese naval forces. To this day it is not known whether such an attack actually took place or whether inexperienced radar operators aboard the two destroyers mistook unidentifiable blips on their radar screens as hostile ships and in response the two U.S. warships began firing at one another.

The North Vietnamese denied taking part in any such naval action, but gunners aboard the U.S. destroyers claimed they sank several attacking small boats. Afterward President Johnson was always evasive about what had actually taken place in the the Gulf of Tonkin, but it was on the basis of this incident, real or imagined, that he asked Congress to pass the so-called Tonkin Gulf Resolution. Congress responded quickly, passing the resolution on August 7, giving Johnson full authority "to take all necessary measures to repel any armed attack against the forces of the United States and to take all measures necessary, including the use of armed force to assist South Vietnam."

This was not an actual declaration of war, but it was the next best thing, and President Johnson and his successor, Richard Nixon, took full advantage of it. It was the basis on which the United States entered and carried on its long war against North Vietnam—the longest war, in fact, in American history.

PRESIDENT JOHNSON ESCALATES THE WAR

By the end of 1964 there were some 25,000 American "advisers" in Vietnam. Actually they were combat troops, and at the beginning of 1965 they were finally allowed officially to take part in combat against the Vietcong. (Most, of course, had already been doing so.) By the spring of 1965 American bombing planes were openly taking part in raids on North Vietnam in an operation called Rolling Thunder. Johnson hoped that Rolling Thunder would so severely punish the North Vietnamese that Ho Chi Minh would be driven to the bargaining table. But no such result was forthcoming, and soon the buildup of American ground forces began.

A U.S. "adviser" with a
South Vietnamese soldier, 1964.
The role of "advisers" in the
war was to expand dramatically
during Johnson's administration.

American planes being readied
to take part in the first
Rolling Thunder mission, 1965

It had been amply demonstrated in World War II that conventional bombing of civilian populations increased rather than decreased their will to resist. But Johnson and the Joint Chiefs of Staff evidently thought that this war would be different. They were wrong. This mistaken belief that America's superior firepower and the advanced mechanization of its armed forces would simply overwhelm the militarily primitive North Vietnamese gave Americans a false anticipation of victory right up to the point where they lost the war.

On March 8, 1965, the first U.S. Marines landed in South Vietnam. Their announced purpose was to protect a U.S. air base at a place called Da Nang. The Marines were followed by paratroopers from the U.S. Army's 173rd Airborne Brigade, and in midsummer President Johnson announced that he had also ordered the First Cavalry Airmobile Division "and certain other forces" to Vietnam. This brought America's troop commitment in Vietnam to 125,000 men, with the end obviously nowhere in sight.

Johnson concluded his announcement with the chilling words, "Additional forces will be needed, and they will be sent as requested." Now the president was no longer trying to keep the war a secret. By the end of 1965 some 200,000 U.S. combat troops were supporting ARVN forces in their battles against the Vietcong. Soon the Vietnam War would become a virtually exclusive U.S. conflict—a conflict that Commander-in-Chief Lyndon Johnson was determined to win at all costs. "I will not be the first American President to lose a war," he bluntly told the American people.

*The first U.S. Marines
landing at Da Nang, 1965.
Friendly South Vietnamese
put garlands of flowers, or
"leis," around their necks.*

3

FIGHTING THE VIETNAM WAR

The Vietnam conflict was America's first teenage war. The average age of all of the U.S. combat soldiers was barely nineteen as opposed to 26 in World War II. Many were just out of high school or high-school dropouts. Few enlisted men were college graduates or even college students. College students were not subject to the draft, thus many young men who were financially able to do so continued their advanced education as long as the war lasted. Far more whites than blacks could afford a college education, which meant that many more blacks than whites were drafted and sent to Vietnam.

A normal tour of duty for draftees in Vietnam was one year. This regulation had been made for morale purposes, but as the war continued it actually did much to harm morale. Units that had lived, trained, and fought together were frequently broken up, inexperienced replacements taking over from experienced combat soldiers. Veteran ''grunts,'' as the infantrymen called themselves, resented the newcomers, and the inexperienced newcomers all too often got themselves killed before anybody in their unit even knew who they were.

In most earlier American wars infantry units trained together and went into combat together. They also remained together until they were wounded or killed or until the conflict ended. In World War II, for example, the 1st Infantry Division—proudly

Men of the 173rd Airborne Brigade on a jungle patrol in South Vietnam's Phuoc Tuy Province. In the background, an armored personnel carrier provides security at the landing zone.

Soldiers resting on armored vehicles during a jungle patrol. Unlike all earlier wars, the Vietnam War was not fought at the front lines. Danger could lurk everywhere—in the jungle, cities, and villages.

A Vietcong prisoner being taken out of his hut. South Vietnamese troops had found a cache of weapons hidden there.

An Australian soldier walking along part of the Ho Chi Minh Trail. Some Australian troops were fighting in Vietnam as part of the Southeast Asia U.S.–Australian defense treaty. The soldier walks on strips built by the Vietcong to make walking up and down hills easier. The log strips were placed at one-stride intervals.

known as The Big Red One by its members—trained in the United States and fought together from the beaches of Normandy to the borders of Germany. Although such prolonged combat resulted in unequal risks for the infantrymen compared with rear-echelon soldiers, morale in such units was extremely high.

Among the U.S. Marines, Air Force, and all U.S. officers in Vietnam, the situation was considerably different. Marines and flyers were volunteers, so their attitude about volunteering for second (and even third) tours of combat duty was considerably different from that of draftee grunts. Officers were required to serve less time than enlisted men in combat in Vietnam—usually only six months before returning home or to "the world," as the grunts called it. This caused resentment on the part of enlisted men, and the frequent changes in leadership also hurt troop morale. As the war progressed and frustration grew among the enlisted men, there were occasional cases of "fragging" of officers. This meant throwing live fragmentation grenades into officers' quarters. As the war progressed, too, the use of narcotics by men at all levels in all of the services became widespread. Narcotics were readily and cheaply available in such cities as Saigon, and from there they found their way into combat areas.

But the greatest enemy of American military morale was the kind of war they had to fight against the Vietcong. For the Americans faced exactly the same problem the French had had in trying to defeat the Vietminh. The enemy refused to stand and fight any major set-piece battles, resorting instead to guerrilla warfare.

Most of the Vietcong were, of course, former Vietminh who had lost none of their guerrilla skills when they underwent a change in name. Regular North Vietnamese army units also began arriving in South Vietnam in the spring of 1965, but they were few in number. Trained in traditional warfare, the North Vietnamese regulars did not play a major role in the fighting in South Vietnam until 1968 and 1969, during and after the Tet Offensive, which actually marked the beginning of the end for the United States in Vietnam.

Meanwhile, some 250,000 Vietcong carried on their relentless guerrilla warfare against the American and ARVN forces, which together outnumbered the Vietcong by as much as three to one. But sheer numbers and superior firepower had little to do with winning guerrilla victories. This was a lesson the Americans had to learn through costly experience. When they did so, they became as successful at jungle warfare as their deadly enemy.

American combat troops soon recognized the similarity between Vietcong tactics and those of the Indians against the U.S. cavalry on the western plains a century earlier. Although that conflict had taken place long before the American soldiers in Vietnam were born, they had heard and read about it as youngsters and seen it reenacted in hundreds of movies as well as on television. Soon they began to refer to the vast Vietnamese jungles where Vietcong guerrillas lurked as "Indian country." Updating the cavalrymen's brutal comment, "the only good Indian is a dead Indian," most Vietnam grunts believed that "the only good Cong is a dead Cong." Frequently the enemy was also called Charlie or Victor Charlie (for the initials of *Viet* and *Cong*). The grunts often called all Vietnamese—both ARVN soldiers and Vietcong—"gooks."

STYLE OF WARFARE IN VIETNAM INDIAN COUNTRY

Indian country, or the enemy-occupied jungle in Vietnam, held not only the threat of sudden ambush but also murderous traps set by the Vietcong. Among these were simple tripwires strung across a trail. When struck by the foot of a soldier on patrol, the wires automatically exploded several nearby hand grenades. Others were balls of mud filled with razor-sharp pieces of bamboo called "punji sticks." These were suspended over jungle trails and swung down to strike passing patrols when triggered by tripwires.

Poisoned punji sticks, their points sharp enough to penetrate U.S. army boots, were also implanted in the earth along jungle trails. In addition, the Vietcong dug actual pits in the ground, lining the bottoms with punji sticks and covering the open tops with branches and jungle brush. Before the war

Two Vietcong sympathizers preparing a spiked bamboo weapon to drop on the enemy as he approaches along a jungle trail.

Village guerrillas laying spiked bamboo traps outside a village. The spikes prevented helicopters from landing.

Traps set in a village to capture unwary soldiers.

such pits had been used to trap and kill wild animals. Now they were used to trap and kill unwary Americans who fell into them and were impaled on the spearlike bamboo stakes at the bottom. Flooded rice fields were another favorite place for punji sticks. Unsuspecting soldiers wading across a rice field could not see the murderous sticks beneath the water and frequently stepped on them.

Village huts were often booby-trapped with grenades and land mines, so Americans learned to approach them warily. The villagers themselves, including women and children, were sometimes used as decoys. Many villagers sympathized with the Vietcong and were willing to aid them against the Americans.

Early in the war American soldiers approached apparently friendly villagers only to find them armed with hand grenades, which they tossed as they fled. Beneath many village huts were openings into tunnels that frequently honeycombed the entire surrounding area. After tossing their grenades at the American soldiers, the villagers might dash into their huts, disappear into these tunnels, and make their way to the protection of the nearby jungle.

In time this kind of warfare resulted in equally savage reactions by the Americans. Grunts learned to shoot first and ask questions later. They also burned down entire Vietnamese villages whose inhabitants were suspected Vietcong sympathizers. Village huts made of bamboo, their roofs thatched with dried jungle vegetation, burned quite readily when set afire by grunts' cigarette lighters. American photographers and news teams were occasionally on the scene when such arson took place and these "Zippo brigade" tactics produced strong reactions when they were shown on TV newscasts. In the comfort of their living rooms, American viewers had little knowledge of what had provoked these actions.

THE MY LAI MASSACRE

Justified or not, however, eventually the grunts' callous treatment of villagers and their homes led to a particularly barbaric incident called the My Lai massacre. On March 16, 1968, Army Lieutenant William L. Calley and some twenty-five soldiers of his platoon not only set fire to the village of My Lai but also allegedly gunned down between 175 and 400 women, children, and old men who were living there.

Right: "Grunts" on patrol. One soldier uses a metal detector to locate land mines. Below: Vietcong prisoners being led by ropes around their necks. Facing page: a U.S. Marine uses a flame-thrower to burn weeds on the edge of a fighting zone. The aim of clearing the area was to prevent sneak attacks by the Vietcong, who would use the tall grass as cover. Flame-throwers were also used directly against the enemy, especially in tunnels and caves.

Some of the massacred
villagers of My Lai, 1968

The village was a suspected Vietcong stronghold, and when they found no Cong in it Calley's platoon—which had suffered many casualties in earlier guerrilla warfare—went berserk and began to get revenge by killing the people they *did* find. Lieutenant Calley was later returned to the United States and charged with his part in the massacre. A court-martial sentenced him to life imprisonment, but his term was later reduced to twenty years.

In fact, Calley did not serve any time in jail. After forty months of confinement to quarters at a U.S. Army post—a privilege granted him by President Nixon—Calley was freed by a federal judge who threw out his conviction. None of the other twenty-five soldiers allegedly involved were ever convicted. According to numerous rumors there were other such mass slayings during the war, but the My Lai incident was the only one to make the headlines.

FREE FIRE ZONES AND SEARCH-AND-DESTROY MISSIONS

The U.S. top military command never really gave up on its belief that superior American technology, manpower, and firepower would eventually defeat the Vietcong. As a result, various tactics were used against the elusive enemy. Two of these were the so-called Free Fire Zones and search-and-destroy missions.

Not only did American soldiers have trouble distinguishing between friendly and unfriendly civilians, they also had trouble distinguishing between actual Vietcong guerrillas and civilians. To grunts all Vietnamese looked alike, and to complicate matters further, guerrillas and civilians frequently dressed alike in pajamalike clothing and sandals. Innocent-looking farmers working in a field might suddenly turn into armed guerrillas when an American patrol came within firing distance or passed them to become vulnerable to surprise attack from the rear.

To eliminate such situations the top U.S. commanders publicly declared that certain areas of the countryside were Free Fire Zones. Anything moving within those areas would be shot, machine-gunned, or bombed by artillery or aircraft. Not all the farmers in the Free Fire Zones were warned of this policy. As a result, numerous innocent peasants as well as their animals were eliminated. Animals, especially oxen for plowing, were extremely valuable to the Vietnamese peasants. Without oxen crops could not be planted or cultivated.

Search-and-destroy missions were somewhat similar, although no prior warnings were given at all. If an American patrol was fired on by snipers from a particular village, the entire village was destroyed. Elsewhere the Americans went looking for enemy opposition from a particular village or area, and when they found it the entire area for miles around was subjected to massive artillery attack or aerial bombardment.

ARVN soldiers rarely wanted to take part in search-and-destroy missions. American soldiers believed that ARVN soldiers avoided them out of cowardice. "When you've got ARVN gooks along," one American sergeant commented to reporters, "it's more like a 'search and disappear' mission—the gooks disappear when they take a shot or two or hear an incoming round."

It may have been true that ARVN soldiers did not relish guerrilla warfare, but they also objected strongly to the indiscriminate killing of soldiers and civilians—political friends and foes—alike. They were also aware that saturation bombing or napalming (napalm was a jellied explosive that burst into flame as soon as it hit an object or the ground) destroyed farmland for months to come. Such raids drove thousands of local peasants into refugee camps outside Saigon and other South Vietnamese cities, and these refugees further complicated the food problem.

Despite the legitimacy of their objections, ARVN troops gradually gained the reputation of being generally unreliable, and more and more U.S. combat units assumed the job of fighting the war themselves.

AGENT ORANGE The American use of poisonous chemical sprays proved to be a further setback to South Vietnamese farmers. These sprays, or defoliants, killed not only all the leaves on trees but also crops growing in the fields. The main defoliant, Agent Orange, was used to kill wide areas of jungle foliage so that the Vietcong could not hide there.

Sprayed from U.S. aircraft (like crop dusting), these defoliants unfortunately fell on troops and civilians in the sprayed areas, or people came into contact with the chemicals after they had been dropped across the countryside. Years after the war numerous American Vietnam veterans became ill with cancer and other diseases allegedly caused by their exposure to Agent Orange. Many of their children were also born with

Members of the 101st Airborne Division move down a hill near Hue on a search and destroy mission. The soldiers look for some 200 Viet-cong who were reported in the area.

Above: *Vietnamese villagers making a stronghold of their village with the assistance of the Vietcong.* Below: *U.S. Marines pour artillery shells into the jungle where they suspect Vietcong troops are hiding.* Facing page: *bombs dropping over North Vietnam. "Charlie" was U.S. soldiers' name for the Vietcong.*

CHOW
CONG CHOW
TO CHARLIE
WITH LOVE

South Vietnamese troops on patrol near Saigon

Napalm exploding on hidden Vietcong military structures. The plane that dropped the bomb can be seen flying away over the center of the white-hot spray.

Refugees from the country-side taking shelter in sewage pipes in Saigon

C-123's of the 12th Air Commando Squadron spraying the jungle with a defoliation liquid. The spray, Agent Orange, defoliated trees that hid Vietcong base areas and communications routes. It also killed crops.

birth defects. (Whether or not this was true—and the probabilities that it was true were strong—the defoliants did destroy almost four million acres of cropland for further use by the Vietnamese peasants for many years.)

After years of litigation, U.S. Vietnam veterans succeeded in obtaining about $200 million from some seven chemical companies that manufactured Agent Orange for use by the armed forces during the war. This out-of-court settlement resulted from a class-action suit by about 250,000 veterans. The companies involved denied all liability for any illnesses the American soldiers suffered from exposure to the deadly defoliants. The settlement granted a top award of about $12,000 to those victims who were totally disabled down to about $3,500 to survivors of veterans who died before January 1, 1985. In addition, the seven chemical companies established a $45 million fund for a foundation to assist Vietnam veterans and their families who claimed disability because of Agent Orange.

THE PHOENIX PROGRAM

The Phoenix program was aimed not at Vietcong guerrillas in the field but directly at the top Vietcong or National Liberation Front (NLF) leadership. A so-called pacification program, Phoenix was actually an assassination program aimed at NLF leaders or suspected leaders. The ''suspected leaders'' category led to widespread killing.

Phoenix was conceived and carried out by members of the U.S. Central Intelligence Agency (CIA). Its leaders were Robert Komer and William Colby, who later became director of the CIA. The idea of the program was to identify and arrest all the undercover NLF officials in villages throughout South Vietnam. Both political and military leaders, many of these officials held relatively minor posts, forming a secret network of underground Communist officials that extended into North Vietnam. If the network could be destroyed, it was believed, the Viet-

A Vietcong prisoner. The Phoenix program was a CIA effort to uproot the Vietcong from the South Vietnamese countryside.

cong guerrillas would find themselves leaderless and thus more readily subject to defeat.

When word went out that the CIA was interested in identifying undercover Vietcong leaders, informers began to turn in names by the score. Some people named suspects because they wanted to gain favor with the Americans; others acted out of spite or desire for revenge. Nevertheless, all suspects were arrested and many were executed. Some were taken to interrogation centers and tortured into admitting NLF connections, and others were caught in their homes and killed.

The Phoenix program continued for two-and-a-half years. When it ended CIA Director Colby told the U.S. Congress that more than 20,000 suspected NLF leaders had been killed through CIA efforts. South Vietnamese officials set the figure at more than 40,000. Whatever the actual "body count", Colby plainly regarded the Phoenix program as a resounding success despite the fact that the wholesale slaughter seemed to have little or no effect on the fighting capability of the Vietcong.

SECRET CIA ACTIVITY IN LAOS

Another CIA "success" story was written in Laos. Laos, of course, was supposed to be out-of-bounds to the American war effort. But beginning in 1962 the CIA entered Laos and enlisted the aid of a few Meo tribesmen and women. Their role was to disrupt traffic along the Ho Chi Minh Trail, down which troops and supplies moved from North Vietnam through a part of Laos and on into South Vietnam.

Starting with a handful of Meo guerrillas, the CIA rapidly built the secret force into an army of thirty thousand men and women. But as the Meo army and its activities expanded, so did the North Vietnamese reaction to it. Soon full-scale war developed between the Meos and the regular North Vietnam military forces, preventing the Meos from achieving their main goal of blocking traffic on the Ho Chi Minh Trail. But the CIA nevertheless regarded its efforts in Laos as well worth the cost of thousands of Meo lives and $30 million American dollars a year.

In the end the Meos, like the Montagnards in South Vietnam, were simply abandoned by the Americans. When the United States gave up the war, what was left of the Meos—perhaps 10,000 out of 250,000 people—fled into neighboring Thailand to avoid total extermination.

Traffic on the Ho Chi Minh Trail

The constant flow of enemy troops and war supplies from North Vietnam into South Vietnam continued to plague the Americans all through the war. This flow occurred not only down the Ho Chi Minh Trail but also in numerous other places along the DMZ. Movement along the Ho Chi Minh Trail was never successfully stopped despite CIA and Meo efforts in Laos and bombing by U.S. B-52 aircraft elsewhere. Along the DMZ the enemy infiltrated almost at will in the face of all U.S. and ARVN efforts to stop them.

Seaborne supplies were fed into North Vietnam from the Soviet Union via Haiphong harbor and by land from China across the North Vietnam–China border. Neither the Soviet Union nor China offered manpower assistance, but as the war progressed both countries furnished important military supplies. President Johnson tried to stop this flow of supplies by ordering bombing raids on North Vietnam, but the U.S. B-52s were ordered to avoid bombing ships in Haiphong harbor for fear of hitting Soviet freighters and tankers. The Johnson administration did not want to provoke the Soviet Union into entering the war, and there was also some fear that China might do so. Both of these fears later proved groundless, but at the time they were genuine.

The B-52s were further hampered in their raids on North Vietnam by modern MiG fighter aircraft supplied by the Soviet Union as well as Soviet-built antiaircraft batteries that fired deadly surface-to-air missiles (SAMs). SAM launching sites were frequently attacked by U.S. bombers, but they were never entirely knocked out and continued to take a heavy toll of American aircraft all through the war. For some curious reason President Johnson would not allow SAM sites to be attacked while they were being built but only after they had begun to launch their missiles. It is possible that he feared killing the Soviet technicians involved in constructing the sites.

Air Force B-52 bombers releasing their bombs. Just three such raids dumped 1.5 million pounds of bombs onto North Vietnamese targets. There were many more equally destructive raids.

On a visit to South Vietnam, U.S. Defense Secretary Robert McNamara concluded that the only way to stop the Vietcong from being reinforced and supplied from the north was to stop infiltration along the DMZ. The way to do this, he thought, was to build an electronic fence all the way across Vietnam. Such a fence would take years to design and more years to build, and it would call for hundreds of thousands of U.S. and ARVN troops to patrol. Nevertheless, scientists in the United States were put to work on the fanciful project, and only after great effort and expense was it abandoned. The fact that it was even considered, however, was a clear indication of how desperate American leaders were to prove the superiority of U.S. technology. Perhaps in the end all such efforts are bound to fail in the face of individual men and women fighting for their freedom.

BODY COUNTS As the war progressed the Vietcong seemed to grow in strength despite their increasing casualties. U.S. forces were also built up until they totaled more than half-a-million men. The growing troop strength on both sides occasionally enabled the United States ground units to engage the Vietcong in traditional infantry battles, and in these the Vietcong always came off second best. In fact, after the Vietnam conflict ended, it was frequently claimed—and these claims were very close to being true—that U.S. forces had won all the battles but lost the war.

About midway through the conflict, American ground commanders believed that the U.S. could defeat the Vietcong in a war of attrition if in no other way. This meant that U.S. manpower and firepower would eventually inflict so many casualties on the Vietcong that they would run out of replacements. As a result of this belief great emphasis began to be placed on so-called body counts.

Body counts eventually became a grisly joke among the American soldiers. Top commanders insisted that all lower units give daily body count reports, and the grunts as well as ARVN troops generously supplied them. The only problem was that these reports were always exaggerated and invariably included all Vietnamese dead—not merely Vietcong guerrillas but also civilian women, children, and old men. Not infrequently a few dead animals were thrown in for good measure. In time, body counts—like McNamara's fanciful fence—were quietly abandoned.

Like the French before them, the Americans could never truly control the rural countryside. By the time the war was several years old, the United States was generally in control of almost all the larger population centers in South Vietnam. But the countryside surrounding these large villages, towns, and cities remained in the hands of the Vietcong guerrillas. From time to time Americans, supported by ARVN troops, might drive the Vietcong completely out of an area. But within a matter of weeks after the Americans withdrew, leaving the ARVN to patrol the "conquered" area, back would come the Vietcong—perhaps only a handful at a time—and eventually the area would once again be in Vietcong hands.

To remedy this frustrating situation U.S. commanders devised what was called the Strategic Hamlet Program. This project was actually a forced resettlement program. A somewhat similar project had been attempted by the South Vietnamese early in the war, but it had been unsuccessful. In given rural areas farmers were moved from the countryside into central fortified villages. Here they would be protected from Vietcong attacks and their needs met through U.S.-supplied goods and food. In the fortified villages the uprooted peasants were also isolated from Vietcong propaganda and recruitment. They could therefore be reeducated along anti-Vietcong, pro-democratic lines.

In fact, the peasants had little interest in political philosophy. All they wanted was to be left alone to follow their traditional way of life. Consequently, this forced resettlement program was doomed to fail almost as soon as it started. The rural farmers freely expressed their violent objections to being uprooted from their ancestral homes and plots of ground to be put into the strategic hamlets, where they were required to earn their daily bread not by growing crops but by helping to build fortifications. The program was struck a further blow by the Vietcong, whose members soon began to infiltrate the strategic hamlets and take advantage of the free food, nightly indoctrination movies, and other American benefits. Since the Americans couldn't tell one Vietnamese from another, weeding out the Vietcong infiltrators was an impossible task.

Meanwhile, the grim war went on. General William Westmoreland, U.S. Commander in Vietnam, continued to call for more troops and gave encouraging reports to President Johnson. Johnson, however, found he was meeting more and more

U.S. tanks on a road with villagers and their oxcart. Vietnamese villagers were caught in the middle of the opposing forces.

General William Westmoreland at the White House in 1967, presenting his request for additional troops to President Johnson and his top advisers

opposition to the war on the home front, not only from the American public but also from some members of his own administration.

From the beginning Johnson had put great faith in the effects of heavy aerial bombardment of North Vietnam. When these bombing efforts failed to bring Ho Chi Minh to the peace table—Ho said he would not talk peace until the Americans got out of Vietnam—Johnson tried periodic halts in the bombing program. When these halts produced no apparent results, the bombing was resumed.

Despite the frustrating lack of progress in the war, by early 1968 the American public had the distinct impression that the scales in the conflict were gradually tipping in the United States' favor. This impression was gained from optimistic statements by Johnson as well as by General Westmoreland, both in Vietnam and in Washington (which he visited several times to appear before Congress). Westmoreland, in fact, said that he "could now see the light at the end of the tunnel"—a phrase that was widely quoted in the press and on television. But at the end of January the light was suddenly put out by a mass attack of Vietcong and North Vietnamese regulars at key spots throughout South Vietnam. This was the historic Tet Offensive.

THE TET OFFENSIVE Tet, the Lunar New Year, had long been a religious holiday in Vietnam. During the war it had been the custom to call a truce to celebrate the occasion. In January 1968 it was generally believed that such a truce would again be declared. But Ho Chi Minh and General Giap had decided to mount a mass offensive against South Vietnam during Tet and thus gain the advantage of surprise.

From a military standpoint the Tet Offensive was at first remarkably successful. And eventually it proved even more successful in destroying America's will to continue the war.

Secretly, General Giap had been preparing the offensive for months. When it was launched, the North Vietnamese regulars and Vietcong guerrillas struck simultaneously at more than thirty South Vietnamese provincial centers, more than sixty towns, and every major city including the capital of Saigon itself.

In Saigon both the American Embassy and South Vietnamese presidential palace were attacked. South of the capital a number of ARVN headquarters were captured. At Cam Ranh Bay and Da Nang major American installations were threatened. Another important base at Khe Sanh, near the DMZ, was also besieged by a force of some 20,000 North Vietnamese regulars and Vietcong guerrillas.

Actually these were exactly the kind of battles the U.S. forces had long been seeking, and General Westmoreland and his commanders wasted no time in taking advantage of the opportunity. In all areas U.S. Army ground troops and Marine infantry struck back in fierce counterattacks, and soon the enemy casualties began to mount.

Within a matter of days Saigon was once again secure, and the ARVN headquarters in the Mekong Delta area were recaptured by U.S. and ARVN forces. The enemy attackers of Khe Sanh were finally driven back, and at Hue a siege situation developed that was to last for two months until the Americans also regained this key strong point. Within a matter of weeks all the towns and cities captured by the enemy in the Tet Offensive had been recaptured. In addition, North Vietnamese casualties amounted to some 45,000 killed and 100,000 wounded, plus 7,000 prisoners of war. ARVN and American casualties, by contrast, came to 4,200 killed and 16,000 wounded.

By any military assessment the United States and ARVN troops had won the Tet Offensive. But as far as the American public was concerned the United States had suffered a terrible defeat.

If Westmoreland had been right about seeing "the light at the end of the tunnel," what was the enemy doing overrunning American installations right in Saigon? And how could North Vietnam mount such a major offensive if it were on the verge of defeat? Perhaps Senator George D. Aiken best summed up the attitude of the American public when he said, "If the Tet Offensive was a failure, I hope the Vietcong never have a major success."

President Johnson recognized the handwriting on the wall. He finally realized that he did not have the essential support of the American public to continue the war. On March 31, 1968, Johnson announced that he would not run for reelection to the presidency that fall. His next move was to recall General Westmoreland from Vietnam and replace him with General Creighton W. Abrams.

*Tet, 1968. Vietcong prepare for the
military offensive that was to take place
at the end of January of that year.*

Khe Sanh, in the northern part of South Vietnam, under siege. Americans at the base were besieged by a massive Communist force early in 1968.

Marines taking cover behind a tank during the siege of Hue, part of the Tet offensive in 1968

The ruins of Hue after the siege of South Vietnam's second most important city. Seventy percent of the houses and shrines in the ancient city were destroyed in the battle.

Fighting during the Tet offensive. One soldier scans the woods while a radio operator tries to make contact with the main force.

On November 6, 1968, Richard M. Nixon was elected president. In an effort to appease the homefront clamor against the Vietnam War, Nixon promised to end the draft and gradually bring home the American troops. But the grim conflict was to go on for several more years. Although Ho Chi Minh died in Hanoi at the age of seventy-nine in the fall of 1969, his immediate successors were pledged to carry on the war until the Americans were driven out of Vietnam. Pham Van Dong, North Vietnam's prime minister, and his aides fully lived up to their pledge.

The Americans were surprised by the strength and intensity of the broad-based Tet attack. The Vietcong surged into more than a hundred cities and towns, including Saigon and Hue. Here, American medics rush the wounded to an aid station.

4

THE WAR ON THE HOME FRONT

The Vietnam War was not only the longest but also the most unpopular war in American history. Home front opposition to it began during the Kennedy administration in the early 1960s and continued to grow until it virtually drove President Johnson out of office in the late 1960s. It remained at a peak of violence during the beginning of President Nixon's first term in office. But when Nixon announced in the early 1970s that he would end the draft and begin bringing the American combat troops home from Vietnam, the antiwar demonstrations began to die out.

The first actual antiwar demonstration was held at the University of Michigan in 1965. That same year there was an antiwar demonstration in Boston, and the first antiwar protest march was made on the nation's Capitol. At the Boston demonstration there were only about 100 protesters. At the same place just four years later 100,000 demonstrators were present. The first march on Washington was made by several thousand students. In November 1969 more than 500,000 people marched on the Capitol demanding an end to the war. This was the largest antiwar protest in U.S. history.

Nevertheless, it should be pointed out that not all demonstrators were opposed to the war. In fact, in 1967 some 750,000 people marched down Fifth Avenue in New York in support of the American soldiers fighting in Vietnam. People in favor of the war were called Hawks. Those who opposed it were called Doves.

GENERAL PUBLIC JOINS STUDENTS IN PEACE MOVEMENT

In the beginning the antiwar movement was mainly headed by student protesters, but soon civilians from all parts of American society joined the movement. When the United States first became actively engaged in the conflict, public opinion polls indicated the majority of Americans were in favor of such action. But by the late 1960s the polls showed a majority of Americans were opposed to continued U.S. participation in the Vietnam War.

As opposition spread, demonstrations were held in numerous cities and on various campuses throughout the country. In 1966 the movement became even more general when so-called International Days of Protest against the U.S. policy in Vietnam were sponsored by American student and nonstudent demonstrators traveling abroad. President Johnson reacted by going on a whirlwind tour of the Far East supposedly to promote peace, and at Christmas he joined with Pope Paul VI in a joint plea for peace in Vietnam.

Returning from his travels, Johnson ordered an increase in the bombing of Hanoi early in 1967. The response to this action was a demonstration by 50,000 peace marchers at the Lincoln Memorial in Washington. The black civil rights leader, Martin Luther King, Jr., also led an anti–Vietnam War march in New York City while a similar protest march took place in San Francisco. The following year King was assassinated in Tennessee, and Robert Kennedy, brother of the slain President John Kennedy, was assassinated in California. Although these murders were not direct results of the war, they seemed to be stark signs of sickness and unrest in American society.

Suspecting that the Soviet Union through its international Communist movement was behind much of the American student protest, the U.S. Federal Bureau of Investigation (FBI) and the CIA began to infiltrate the various protest groups. Leaders' phones were tapped, and protest meetings were photographed by federal agents or local police. Secret intelligence files were also created, containing detailed information about antiwar movement members. All of this intelligence activity was probably illegal, and no proof of any connection with the Soviet Union was ever established.

Some of the most violent and disruptive demonstrations were staged by anti-war protestors at the Democratic political convention held in Chicago in August of 1968. It was at this convention that Hubert H. Humphrey, Vice President under Lyndon Johnson, was nominated to run against the Republican nominee, Richard M. Nixon. In the fall election Nixon defeated Humphrey.

While the Democratic convention was being held the city of Chicago was caught up in serious civil disturbance. Preconvention reports indicated as many as 100,000 anti-war protestors would attempt to disrupt the city's life. As a result, Chicago put its police force on overtime duty, and Illinois alerted the National Guard.

Actually only about 10,000 protesters arrived in Chicago, and they were opposed by some 20,000 law enforcement officers. Nevertheless, there were repeated clashes between the demonstrators and security forces. Several hundred civilians and policemen were injured, and more than 600 protesters were arrested.

Some of the most serious clashes took place in Grant Park where the police tried to confine the protest activity. The anti-war champion among politicians vying for the Democratic presidential nomination was Senator Eugene McCarthy of Minnesota. McCarthy visited with the protesters in Grant Park and made serious efforts to prevent the demonstrations from spilling over into the city's streets and turning into a full-fledged and disastrous riot. Although McCarthy was defeated for the nomination by fellow Minnesotan Humphrey, McCarthy's strong anti-Vietnam War stand greatly influenced the Senate's final stand against continuing the war.

OTHER PROTEST ACTIVITY   The student protesters did more than demonstrate and stage protest marches. Many publicly burned their draft cards or refused to report for induction into the military services when they were drafted. By the late 1960s some 35,000 young Americans had been prosecuted for draft evasion. Many others—perhaps as many as 100,000—fled to Canada or Sweden to avoid conscription. After the war President Jimmy Carter declared an amnesty for all draft evaders who had fled the country during the Vietnam War. This allowed them to return to the United States without fear of prosecution, and many did so. Many others, however, are still living abroad today.

*The 1967 march on the Pentagon
Anti-war demonstrators place flowers
in the gun barrels of military police.*

Anti-war demonstrators
come face-to-face with
Illinois National Guardsmen
outside the Democratic
Convention headquarters
in Chicago, 1968.

Anti-war demonstrators
burning their draft cards
(1970) outside Selective
Service headquarters.
The burning was part of
a week-long nationwide
anti-draft campaign.

Perhaps the most violent form of protest by young Americans was registered by Norman Morrison, a Quaker who burned himself to death before the Pentagon in Washington, D.C. Morrison's act, called self-immolation, was doubtless prompted by similar suicides by the Buddhist monks in Saigon. None of these acts had any effect on American policies.

PROTESTS WITHIN THE MILITARY; CAMPUS SLAYINGS

The antiwar movement was not confined to civilians. Within the military establishment itself there was much antiwar feeling. During the course of the conflict more than 50,000 men deserted the armed services, many of them fleeing the United States after they were inducted but before they were shipped to Vietnam. Returning Vietnam veterans were generally eager to disappear back into civilian life, but many of them also joined the protest movement. To do so they formed their own organization, Vietnam Veterans Against the War. In 1971 they staged a march on Washington, demonstrating their strong antiwar feelings to President Nixon and the nation's legislators by tossing their combat medals at the Capitol.

One of the things the veterans were protesting was the increasing violence with which U.S. law enforcement agencies attempted to stop student antiwar demonstrations. Just a few months earlier, in 1970, two students were killed and several were wounded at Mississippi's Jackson State University when police opened fire on war protesters there. And at Kent State University in Ohio, National Guardsmen had fired on student demonstrators gathered on the campus commons, killing four students and wounding nine others.

NIXON WIDENS THE WAR

When President Nixon took office, he promised to end the war and gain "peace with honor." Actually he and National Security Adviser Henry Kissinger widened the conflict. They did so by approving the invasion of Cambodia and Laos by U.S. and ARVN forces and stepping up the bombing campaign against North Vietnam. The invasions—Nixon referred to them as "incursions"—of neutral Cambodia and Laos were necessary, Nixon and Kissinger insisted, to destroy so-called privileged sanctuaries where North Vietnamese troops had been hiding throughout the war. (No mention was made of secret U.S. operations that had been going on in the two countries all through the war.) The bombing of North Vietnam in ever-increasing fury was supposed to force the enemy to sue for

An anti-war demonstration at Kent State
University in Ohio in 1970 ended in tragedy
when National Guardsmen fired on students.
Four students were killed; nine were wounded.

President Nixon explaining his reasons for sending U.S. troops into Cambodia

American soldiers hauling away a cache of weapons from a North Vietnamese stronghold in Cambodia

peace. Like Johnson, Nixon had blind faith in an ultimate victory produced by U.S. air power. And also like Johnson, Nixon had no intention of being the first U.S. president to lose a war.

Despite Nixon's and Kissinger's explanations, this widening of the war further stirred student violence at home. It also brought strong criticism and threats of legislative action by the U.S. Congress. Although the Tonkin Gulf Resolution had actually been repealed in May of 1970, Nixon continued to act as if it were still in effect.

Nixon did, however, live up to his campaign promises by beginning to reduce American troop levels in Vietnam. At its peak U.S. military strength was about 500,000 men. By early 1972 this number had been reduced to about 160,000 men. Nixon accomplished this reduction in combat forces by a so-called Vietnamization of the war.

Vietnamization simply meant letting more ARVN troops and fewer American troops do the fighting. This could have only one inevitable result—the loss of the war.

5

THE FINAL ACT

As the United States began to withdraw its troops from Vietnam, the North Vietnamese stepped up their military offensive. Because the Vietcong had suffered so many casualties in the Tet Offensive, the North Vietnamese regular army was called on to do much of the fighting against the ARVN forces, who were now supported by the remaining U.S. troops.

In the spring of 1972 the North Vietnamese opened a major offensive. This was called the Easter Offensive, and it made strong gains throughout South Vietnam. But the heavy retaliatory U.S. air raids on Hanoi were also beginning to take their toll, and North Vietnam began to have trouble supplying its forces in the south. In late 1972 Nixon ordered the heaviest air raids of the war; these were called the Christmas bombings. By early 1973 the war had reached a stalemate with neither side able to gain the upper hand.

This stalemate had one good effect. It caused peace talks (which had begun in 1968) to be held in earnest in Paris, where the United States was represented by Henry Kissinger and North Vietnam by Le Duc Tho. On January 27, 1973, a peace agreement, the Paris Accords, was signed. By that spring all the remaining U.S. troops had returned home from Vietnam, with only a few hundred Marine guards left on duty at the U.S. Embassy in Saigon. The draft officially ended in June 1973.

Henry Kissinger, national security adviser to President Nixon, signing the Paris peace accords, 1973. North Vietnam's Le Duc Tho has his back to the camera.

The fall of Saigon, April 1975. South Vietnamese are shown attempting to get into the American Embassy in Saigon. Refugees flowed into the city, fleeing the advance of the Communist forces. Only a few made it into the embassy. Fewer still escaped by helicopter.

But no sooner had the Paris Accords been signed than both sides began violating them, and sporadic fighting continued throughout South Vietnam. Nixon was in favor of resuming the air war against North Vietnam, but at this point the American people and Congress had had enough of the war. In July 1973, Congress voted not only to end all bombing in Vietnam but also to prohibit any future U.S. military action there without congressional approval. Nixon later vetoed this War Powers Act, but on November 7 Congress overrode his veto. The bill still stands today. Nixon continued to ask for financial aid for South Vietnam, but all his requests were sharply reduced by the Congress.

This action restored to Congress its constitutional right to declare war, which had been weakened by the Tonkin Gulf Resolution.

It also effectively took the United States out of the war, although fighting there was to continue for another year and a half. Saigon, the capital of South Vietnam, fell to North Vietnamese and Vietcong forces on April 30, 1975.

The scene at the American Embassy in Saigon on the final day was a sorry one. Much of the action there was shown on American television, and viewers again sat watching in their homes, this time agonizing over the final tragic act in the first war the United States had ever lost.

Rescue helicopters landed at the embassy, took aboard U.S. officials and eleven Marine guards, and carried them to U.S. warships located just offshore in the South China Sea. Some South Vietnamese tried to climb the fences surrounding the embassy grounds, but most were beaten off. Those few who made it inside could be seen clinging to the landing gears of the helicopters as they took off. Others were simply left on the embassy roof or on the embassy grounds.

Some Vietnamese officials and military officers were rescued by helicopters from Saigon or from other nearby airfields, and many escaped by boat. Most, however, like the rest of the South Vietnamese, were left behind to face the conquering enemy.

So many helicopters landed on the decks of the rescue ships that soon there was no more room for them. To make room sailors simply pushed dozens of recently-landed helicopters off the decks and into the ocean. Many millions of dollars worth of choppers were thus discarded.

President Nixon was no longer in office when the end of the war came in Vietnam. He had resigned as president, the first U.S. chief executive to do so, on August 9, 1974. He was succeeded by his Vice President, Gerald R. Ford.

The event that brought about Nixon's downfall was called the "Watergate Affair." Indirectly, however, the Vietnam War was responsible. And leading up to the Watergate Affair was a directly war-related incident, the publication of the so-called Pentagon Papers.

The Pentagon is the pentagon-shaped or five-sided building in Washington that houses the U.S. Department of Defense. One of the people working there during the Vietnam War was a young man named Daniel Ellsberg. As part of his job Ellsberg worked on a lengthy report for Defense Secretary Robert S. McNamara that gave in full detail the complete history of U.S. involvement in the war. One of the things it clearly showed was how much of the conduct of the war was kept secret from the American public.

Ellsberg had started the war as a hawk but gradually he became a dove. And while working on the report for McNamara he became convinced that all of the information in it should be made public. Despite the fact that this report, which soon became known as the Pentagon Papers, was classified as secret, Ellsberg began to "leak" copies of it to the press.

When the Pentagon Papers were published—first by *The New York Times* and then elsewhere—they caused a sensation. Among many other important disclosures, the papers implied that the Gulf of Tonkin incident, which had brought the United States fully into the war, had probably been manufactured by President Johnson. Attempts were made to suppress the Pentagon Papers, but to no avail.

The Nixon Administration then tried to obtain information that would discredit Ellsberg. Nixon and his aides feared that if he were not discredited he might make similarly damning disclosures about Nixon's conduct of the war. Several Nixon aides secretly broke into Ellsberg's psychiatrist's office in Los Angeles. These burglars were called the "Plumbers Unit" because they were supposed to fix leaks of government information. Whatever they hoped to find in this particular burglary was never made clear, but the attempt was unsuccessful.

Gradually the furor over the Pentagon Papers died down, but they were to come back to haunt President Nixon.

When Nixon ran for President in 1972 a second Plumbers Unit burglarized the national headquarters of the Democratic party in Washington. These headquarters were located in a combination apartment and office complex called Watergate. The Plumbers were trying to steal Democratic campaign plans and to plant electronic ''bugs'' in the offices of people who were running the campaign against Nixon.

During the course of the Watergate break-in the burglars were caught. Police did not immediately connect them with the White House, however. In fact it was many months before it became public knowledge that President Nixon and his aides knew about the Watergate break-in shortly after it happened. There were also strong suspicions that the White House had even participated in planning the Plumbers' Watergate operation, but these suspicions were never confirmed.

During the Senate Watergate hearings, which were held to investigate the affair, the public learned that the President himself had tried to cover up his knowledge of the burglary. The earlier burglary of Ellsberg's psychiatrist's office was also disclosed.

Because of these disclosures President Nixon was threatened with impeachment by the Senate. He chose instead to resign as chief executive. Later, his successor, Gerald Ford, issued a full pardon for any questionable acts that Nixon might have committed during his presidency.

AFTERMATH AT HOME

In the United States the immediate aftermath of the Vietnam War was a general feeling of frustration and bitterness. The conflict had divided the country as it had not been divided since the Civil War, and the division remained long after 1975. The nation had spent more than $110 billion and suffered more than 58,000 casualties in dead and missing in action. The unanswerable question was, had there been any point in this vast expenditure of blood and money?

Curiously, the civilian population took out its frustration and bitterness on the returning Vietnam veterans themselves. Always in the past the nation had honored its soldiers returning from the wars, but this time the attitude was different. Somehow, the public seemed to think, the veterans themselves were responsible for the war. As a result, Vietnam veterans were publicly insulted, spat upon, and otherwise reviled and made to feel like outcasts from society.

Above: *photographer posing beside spent shells and a burned-out tank along the road to Quang Tri City.* Center: *President Nixon announcing his resignation, August 8, 1974.* Right: *ex-prisoner of war being greeted by his family*

In response the veterans themselves were at first bewildered and then openly resentful. They hadn't expected to be hailed as conquering heroes, but they did expect to have their efforts and sacrifice understood and respected. Many of them had survived the hell of the jungle fighting in Vietnam with only their thoughts of home—the "real world"—to sustain them. Returning home to a world they no longer knew and a hostile public that wanted nothing to do with them (many veterans were refused jobs when prospective employers learned they had been in the war) sent numerous returnees into states of deep depression.

Veterans returning from wars have always had difficulty in readjusting to civilian life. Vietnam veterans had more trouble than most. The incidence among them of nervous breakdowns, alcoholism, drug addiction, and just plain failure to adjust to the workaday world was abnormally high. In addition, many of them suffered from lingering illnesses acquired during the war.

To make matters worse, the U.S. Veterans Administration was none too sympathetic in treating chronically ill Vietnam veterans and was positively stubborn in its refusal to grant them even partial disabilities, which would have made them eligible for pensions.

All in all, the lot of the returning Vietnam War veterans was far from a happy one for many years.

AFTERMATH ABROAD

In both North and South Vietnam the severe suffering from widespread death and destruction also lingered long after the war. More than 200,000 ARVN soldiers were killed, and about 500,000 were wounded in the war. Another 500,000 South Vietnamese civilians were killed and at least 1,000,000 wounded.

North Vietnamese casualties were even higher, with an estimated one million soldiers killed and as many as three million wounded. The number of civilian deaths in North Vietnam is not known.

It is also not known how many people died in Laos and Cambodia during the conflict, although they must number in the hundreds of thousands. The total war dead have been estimated at more than four million, and the total cost of the war has been estimated at perhaps $500 billion. The actual figures will never be known.

When the North Vietnamese took over Saigon they renamed it Ho Chi Minh City. Former South Vietnamese officials and army officers were arrested and sent to so-called reeducation camps. Here they were taught the Communist philosophy of government, with the promise of release back into civilian life as soon as they had achieved the "proper attitude." Far from all were released. As late as the mid-1980s the reeducation camps still held as many as 10,000 political prisoners.

North and South Vietnam were officially merged into one country in 1976. Although there is peace throughout the country now, Vietnam remains a troubled nation. Many of its ills are economic, since Vietnam is one of the poorest countries in the world. Because of the poverty and because they did not want to live in a Communist police state, more than a million people fled the country after the war. Many fled to Thailand, making the risky journey through Laos and Cambodia, which has been renamed Kampuchea. Others took even greater risks by escaping in fishing boats and other small craft into the dangerous South China Sea. These "boatpeople" hoped to be picked up by U.S. Navy ships and other friendly vessels. Another half-a-million people have applied to leave the country legally, but only a few are allowed to leave each week. Many of these emigrants have settled in the United States.

The government of Communist Vietnam insists that President Nixon promised that the United States would pay some $3.25 billion in economic development funds once peace came. If this promise was made, it has never been kept, and there is little likelihood that it will be.

Vietnam has reluctantly been returning the remains of some of the 1,820 Americans who were missing in action during the war. It did return what it claimed were all the U.S. prisoners of war, but there have been persistent rumors that U.S. POWs are still being held in secret jungle camps—perhaps in Laos— by the vindictive Vietnamese government.

AMERASIAN CHILDREN

Perhaps one of the greatest lingering tragedies of the Vietnam War is the large number of so-called Amerasian children left behind by the departing American forces. These children were born as a result of love affairs between American service men and Vietnamese women. Most of the mothers and fathers of these children were not married, and when the war ended the fathers simply abandoned their illegitimate offspring and returned to the United States. Even many of the Americans who did marry their Vietnamese sweethearts eventually abandoned both their wives and children.

The tragedy involved in this aspect of the war's aftermath is that the Amerasian children have not been accepted by the rest of Vietnamese society. The children have become complete outcasts who are forced to beg in the streets in order to stay alive. Some efforts have been made by the U.S. government as well as by welfare organizations to reunite these broken families, but many hundreds of Amerasian children still roam the streets of Vietnamese cities.

CAMBODIA'S ORDEAL Cambodia suffered an even greater ordeal than Vietnam in the aftermath of the war. The U.S. invasion there upset the political balance and caused a revolution that threatened the extinction of the Cambodians as a people. The country was taken over by a revolutionary despot named Pol Pot and renamed Kampuchea. Pol Pot's forces—the Khmer Rouge— were a terrorist organization that wanted to return the country to the most basic form of existence. Hundreds of thousands of educated and semieducated Cambodians were killed—even wearing glasses could result in a death sentence—and many thousands more were driven from the country.

At the height of the Khmer Rouge madness the Vietnamese invaded the country. But they also treated the Cambodians brutally, allowing many of those who had not been killed by the Khmer Rouge to starve to death and putting many others in reeducation camps. The Vietnamese were not so much interested in saving Cambodian lives as they were in gaining control of the country.

During the decade following the end of the Vietnam War it is estimated that some four million Cambodians out of an original population of eight million had been killed, starved to death, or fled the country. In the mid-1980s the Vietnamese still had more than 200,000 troops in Kampuchea, which had become a police state. Some Western observers doubted that Kampuchea/Cambodia, whose history extends back to ancient times, could long survive as a nation and a people.

THE SOVIETS IN VIETNAM While much of Indochina's future continued in doubt, the Soviet Union took advantage of the turmoil and began to establish military bases in Vietnam. One of the most important

Facing page: *''boat people'' escaping Vietnam by sea. Many died during the ordeal. More than 700,000 Indochinese refugees have been admitted to the United States since 1975.*

Above left: *wounded North Vietnamese soldiers.* Above right: *South Vietnamese officers undergoing reeducation by North Vietnamese military.* Left: *a thirteen-year-old Amerasian girl attending school in Vietnam. Some efforts have been made to reunite Amerasian children with their fathers in the United States.*

of these was at Cam Ranh Bay, the former major U.S. base. In general the Vietnamese did not welcome the presence of the Russians in their midst any more than they had welcomed the French, Japanese, or Americans. But the Soviets continued to supply much-needed economic aid to the Vietnamese, so their presence had to be more-or-less tolerated.

The establishment of the Soviet military base at Cam Ranh Bay was, of course, bad news for U.S. long-range military planners. It made the whole of Indochina vulnerable to the Russians as it had never been before. The loss of the Vietnam War was more keenly felt by the United States in this than in any other way. It also heightened the need for reestablishing China as a close ally and for continued close relations with the Republic of the Philippines. The loss of either of these two as potential or actual military bases would also threaten the loss of the whole Pacific Basin area.

BINDING UP THE WOUNDS AT HOME

Meanwhile, at home, Americans began the more constructive process of binding up the wounds of the Vietnam War. In 1979 President Jimmy Carter announced the first Vietnam Veterans' Week, to be observed in late May. "The nation still has a moral debt to these boys who served in Southeast Asia," President Carter said. "It is time to recognize Vietnam-era veterans for their heroic service."

General recognition by the public came slowly. Jan C. Scruggs and Robert Donbek founded the Vietnam Veterans Memorial fund to gather money for a Vietnam memorial to veterans to be erected in Washington. John Wheeler was also involved in this fund-raising effort. A contest was also held to decide who should design the memorial. The contest was won by Maya Ying Lin, a Chinese-American Yale University student.

At first Lin's design caused much controversy. It was a simple, slender black granite wall sunk into the ground at an angle on a gently rising slope. On this shiny black wall were inscribed the names of all the more than 58,000 American dead and missing from the Vietnam War. Critics of the memorial objected to its stark simplicity, claiming that it was not a fitting tribute to the men whose names it bore.

The Lin-designed memorial was dedicated in 1982. As a concession to its critics a more conventional sculpture was added to the site in 1984. Sculpted by Frederick Hart, this

A veteran touches the memorial to 58,022 Americans killed or missing in Indochina. At the end of 1985, the Pentagon decided to add 96 more names to the memorial. The new names are of those killed in combat-related activities such as crash landings or accidental bomb explosions.

depicts three U.S. soldiers cast in bronze. The figures are shown wearing combat fatigues and carrying automatic weapons. They stare with a steady, lost gaze at the nearby wall.

The two elements of the Vietnam War Veterans Memorial complement one another, but it is toward the wall that visitors move as if drawn by a magnet. And, confounding the early critics, visitors come by the millions. In the mid-1980s more than two million visitors a year came to see it, making it the most frequently visited monument in Washington. They come silently, reverently, many bearing flowers. They stand before it like worshipers.

John Wheeler, a leader of the veterans' organization that made the memorial possible, commented about the wall's effect on veterans visiting it: "The actual act of being at the Memorial is healing for the guy or woman who went to Vietnam. It has to do with the felt presence of comrades."

But civilians, too—nonveterans who once criticized or protested against the Vietnam War and reviled its participants—have been healed by their visits to the memorial. The somber black wall, with its grim honor roll of those who gave their lives in Vietnam, has become a symbol of the nation's binding up its wounds and coming together again so many long years after the end of that terrible conflict.

*Veterans of the Vietnam War
marching in a ticker-tape parade
in New York City, 1985, ten
years after the fall of Saigon and
the end of the war in Vietnam*

INDEX

Abrams, Creighton W., 56
Agent Orange, 40, 45, 47
Aiken, George D., 56
Amerasian children, 78–79, 81
American advisers, 13, 16, 24
American Embassy, 55, 73
American public, 14, 55–56
Amnesty, 64
Antiwar demonstrations, 62–66
    burning draft cards, 66
    Kent State University, 68
    march on the Pentagon, 65
Antiwar feeling, 55
    opinion polls, 63
    within military establishment, 67
Army of the Republic of Vietnam, 13

Boatpeople, 78, 80
Bodycounts, 52
Bombing, 43, 50
    civilian populations, 27
    Congress, 73
    saturation, 40
Buddhists, 13, 17, 19, 67

C. Turner Joy, 24
Calley, William L., 35, 39
Cam Ranh Bay, 56, 82
Cambodia, 1–2, 67, 69, 77–79

Carter, Jimmy, 64, 82
Charlie, 32, 43
China, 7, 51, 82
Chopper war, 14
Christmas bombings, 71
CIA, 17, 63
    Ho Chi Minh Trail, 51
    Laos, 48
    the Phoenix program, 46–48
    protest groups, 63
Colby, William, 47–48
Communists
    American student protests, 63
    police state, 78
    secret network, 47
Congress, 24
    Westmoreland, 55
    Tonkin Gulf Resolution, 20
    War Powers Act, 73
Counter-insurgency activity, 14

Da Nang, 27, 56
De Castries, Christian, 4
Defoliants, 40, 45, 47
Democratic Republic of Vietnam, 2
Diem, Ngo Dinh, 12–14, 17, 19–20, 23
Dien Bien Phu, 3–10
DMZ, 10, 51–52, 56

Domino theory, 7, 20
Donbek, Robert, 82
Dong, Pham Van, 61
Doves, 63, 74
Draft, 28
    amnesty, 64
    burning draft cards, 64
    evasion, 64
    Nixon, Richard M., 61
Dragon Lady, 17
DRV, 2, 13
Dulles, John Foster, 9

Easter Offensive, 71
Eisenhower, Dwight D., 7, 9–10, 13–14, 20
Elections, 10, 13
Ellsberg, Daniel, 74–75
Ely, Paul, 9

FBI, 63
Ford, Gerald R., 74–75
Fragging, 31
France, 1–6, 9–10, 14, 31, 53
Free Fire Zones, 39
French Indochina War, 3, 6
Fulbright, 21

Geneva, 13–14
Giap, Vo Nguyen, 2–6, 9, 14, 55
Gooks, 32
Grant Park, 64
Green Berets, 14, 23
    Laos, 17
    Montagnards, 17
Grunts, 28, 31–32, 35, 37, 39, 52
Gulf of Tonkin, 23–24, 74

Haiphong harbor, 51
Hanoi, 2, 6, 13, 61, 63, 71
Hawks, 63, 74
Herrick, John J., 23–24
Ho Chi Minh, 2, 5, 7, 9–10, 13–14, 24, 55, 61
Ho Chi Minh City, 78
Ho Chi Minh Trail, 21, 30, 48–49, 51
Hue, 41, 56, 58–60
Humphrey, Hubert H., 64

Incursions, 67
Indian country, 32
Indochina, 2, 6–7, 9, 79, 82
International Days of Protest, 63

International peace conference, 10
Interrogation centers, 48

Jackson State University, 67
Johnson, Lyndon B., 20–21, 23–25, 27, 51, 55–56, 62–64, 70, 74
    emergency powers, 23
    Gulf of Tonkin, 23–24, 74
    Westmoreland, William, 53–56

Kampuchea, 1, 78–79
Kennedy, John F., 14, 16–17, 20, 62–63
Kennedy, Robert, 63
Kent State University, 67–68
Khe Sanh, 56, 58
Khmer Rouge, 79
King, Martin Luther, Jr., 63
Kissinger, Henry, 67, 70–72
Komer, Robert, 47

Land reform, 17
Langlais, Pierre, 4
Laos, 1–2, 4, 17, 48, 51, 67, 77–78
Le Duc Tho. *See* Tho, Le Duc
Lunar New Year, 55

Maddox, 23–24
Marines, 26–27, 31, 36, 42, 71
    siege of Hue, 58
    Tet Offensive, 56
McCarthy, Eugene, 64
McNamara, Robert, 16, 51–52, 74
Mekong Delta, 13, 16, 56
Meo, 48, 51
Montagnards, 17–18, 48
Morale, 28, 31
Morrison, Norman, 67
My Lai, 35, 38

Napalm, 40, 44
Narcotics, 31
National Guard, 64, 66–68
National Liberation Front, 14, 47
Navarre, Henri, 4
Ngo Dinh Diem. *See* Diem, Ngo Dinh
Ngo Dinh Nhu. *See* Nhu, Ngo Dinh
Nguyen Van Thieu. *See* Thieu, Nguyen Van
Nhu, Ngo Dinh, 17–18
    Madame Nhu, 17–19
Nixon, Richard M., 20, 24, 39, 61–62, 64, 67, 69–76, 78

NLF, 14, 47–48

Pacific Basin area, 82
Pacification program, 47
Paris Accords, 71–73
Peace marchers, 63
Peace talks, 71
Pentagon, 65, 74, 83
Pentagon Papers, 74
Pham Van Dong. *See* Dong, Pham
  Van
Phoenix Program, 46–48
Phuoc Tuy Province, 29
Plumbers Unit, 74–75
Poisonous chemical sprays, 40
Pol Pot, 79
Political prisoners, 78
Psychological weapons, 6
Pungi sticks, 32, 35

Quang Tri City, 76

Red River delta, 13
Reeducation camps, 78–79
Refugees, 10, 12–13, 40, 45, 72,
  80
Republic of the Philippines, 82
Resettlement, 53
Rice bowl, 13
Rolling Thunder, 24–25
Rusk, Dean, 16

Saigon, 12, 17, 40, 44–45, 60, 67,
  72–73, 78, 84
    Narcotics, 31
    Tet Offensive, 55–56
Scruggs, Jan C., 82
Search-and-destroy missions, 39–41
Self-immolation, 67
South China Sea, 6, 73, 78
Southeast Asia U.S.–Australian De-
  fense treaty, 30
Soviets, 7, 51, 63, 82

Strategic Hamlet Program, 53
Students, 28, 63–64, 67, 70

Teenage war, 28
Tet Offensive, 31, 55–56, 58–59, 71
Thailand, 6, 48, 78
Thieu, Nguyen Van, 23
Tho, Le Duc, 71–72
Tonkin Gulf Resolution, 20, 24, 70,
  73
Truman, Harry S, 7, 20

U.S. Central Intelligence Agency
  (CIA), 17, 47–48
U.S. Federal Bureau of Investigation
  (FBI), 63
U.S. Veterans Administration, 77

Victor Charlie, 32
Vietcong
    bodycount, 52
    Indian country, 32
    Phoenix program, 47–48
    sympathizers, 33
    Tet Offensive, 55–56
    Traps, 33, 35
Vietminh, 2–3, 7, 11, 14, 31
    Dien Bien Phu, 8
    French, 2–9, 14
Vietnam Independence League, 2
Vietnam Veterans' Week, 82
Vietnamization, 70
Vo Nguyen Giap. *See* Giap, Vo
  Nguyen

War dead, 77
War Powers Act, 73
Watergate, 74–75
Westmoreland, William, 53–56
Wheeler, John, 82, 85
World War II, 1–2, 4, 28, 31

Zippo Brigade, 35